Create a cheery nursery with color-block blankets. The 6 crochet designs in this book feature a mix of stripes, motifs, and other patterns in medium weight yarn.

LEISURE ARTS, INC. • Maumelle, Arkansas

NINE-COLOR combo

BEGINNER

Finished Size: 30" x 43" (76 cm x 109 cm)

SHOPPING LIST

Yarn (Medium Weight) MEDIUM 4

[6 ounces, 315 yards

(170.1 grams, 288 meters) per skein]:

- ☐ Dk Rose - 1 skein
- ☐ Strawberry - 1 skein
- ☐ Purple - 1 skein
- ☐ Off White - 1 skein
- ☐ Lavender - 1 skein
- ☐ Blue - 1 skein
- ☐ Lime Green - 1 skein
- ☐ Dk Peach - 1 skein
- ☐ Yellow - 1 skein

Crochet Hook

- ☐ Size K (6.5 mm)

  or size needed for gauge

Additional Supplies

- ☐ Yarn needle

GAUGE INFORMATION

11 dc and 6 rows = 4" (10 cm)

Gauge Swatch: 4" (10 cm) square

With Dk Rose, ch 13.

Row 1: Dc in fourth ch from hook **(3 skipped chs count as first dc)** and in each ch across: 11 dc.

Rows 2-6: Ch 3 **(counts as first dc)**, turn; dc in next dc and in each dc across.

Finish off.

PANELS #1 & #5

With Dk Rose, ch 25.

Row 1 (Right side)**:** Dc in fourth ch from hook **(3 skipped chs count as first dc, now and throughout)** and in each ch across: 23 dc.

Note: Loop a short piece of yarn around any stitch to mark Row 1 as **right** side.

Rows 2-6: Ch 3 **(counts as first dc, now and throughout)**, turn; dc in next dc and in each dc across; at end of Row 6, change to Strawberry in last dc ***(Fig. 3b, page 22)***.

Rows 7-22: Ch 3, turn; dc in next dc and in each dc across; at end of Row 22, change to Dk Peach in last dc.

Rows 23-28: Ch 3, turn; dc in next dc and in each dc across; at end of Row 28, change to Yellow in last dc.

Rows 29-44: Ch 3, turn; dc in next dc and in each dc across.

Finish off.

PANELS #2 & #4

With Lime Green, ch 26.

Row 1 (Right side)**:** Dc in fourth ch from hook and in each ch across: 24 dc.

Note: Mark Row 1 as **right** side.

Rows 2-12: Ch 3, turn; dc in next dc and in each dc across; at end of Row 12, change to Blue in last dc.

Rows 13-18: Ch 3, turn; dc in next dc and in each dc across; at end of Row 18, change to Purple in last dc.

Rows 19-30: Ch 3, turn; dc in next dc and in each dc across; at end of Row 19, change to Off White in last dc.

First Half

Row 1: Ch 3, turn; dc in next 11 dc, leave remaining 12 dc unworked: 12 dc.

Rows 2-14: Ch 3, turn; dc in next dc and in each dc across.

Finish off.

Second Half

Row 1: With **right** side facing, join Lavender with dc in first unworked dc after First Half ***(see Joining With Dc, page 21)***; dc in next dc and in each dc across: 12 dc.

Complete same as First Half; leave a long end for sewing when finishing off.

Thread yarn needle with long end and sew end of rows of Halves together.

PANEL #3

With Yellow, ch 25.

Row 1 (Right side)**:** Dc in fourth ch from hook and in each ch across: 23 dc.

Note: Mark Row 1 as **right** side.

Rows 2-20: Ch 3, turn; dc in next dc and in each dc across; at end of Row 20, change to Dk Rose in last dc.

Rows 21-26: Ch 3, turn; dc in next dc and in each dc across; at end of Row 26, change to Dk Peach in last dc.

Rows 27-38: Ch 3, turn; dc in next dc and in each dc across; at end of Row 38, change to Strawberry in last dc.

Rows 39-44: Ch 3, turn; dc in next dc and in each dc across.

Finish off.

ASSEMBLY

With **right** side of all Panels facing and using Placement Diagram as a guide, sew Panels together with corresponding colors.

PLACEMENT DIAGRAM

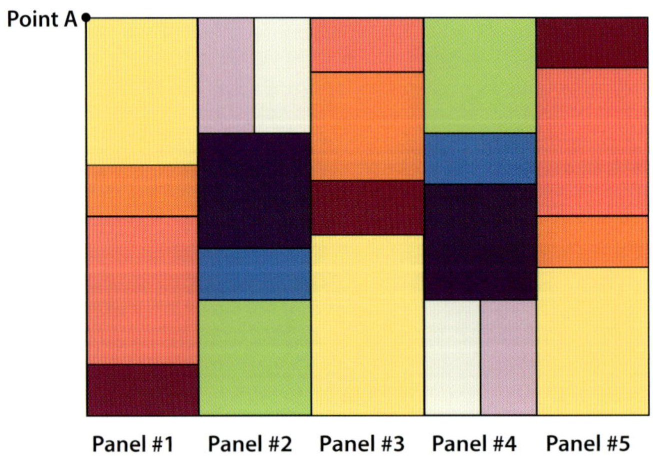

EDGING

With **right** side facing, join Off White with slip st in end of Row 1 of Panel #1 (Point A); ch 3, ★ (slip st in end of next row, ch 3) across; working in dc and in free loops of beginning chs ***(Fig. 2, page 21)*** across Panels, (slip st, ch 3) twice in first st, skip next st, (slip st in next st, ch 3, skip next st) across to last st, (slip st, ch 3) twice in last st; repeat from ★ once **more**; join with slip st to joining slip st, finish off.

EASY

Finished Size: 30" x 38½" (76 cm x 98 cm)

COLORFUL subway

SHOPPING LIST

Yarn (Medium Weight) 4

[5 ounces, 256 yards (141 grams, 234 meters) per skein]:

- ☐ Off White - 2 skeins
- ☐ Blue/Green - 1 skein
- ☐ Coral - 1 skein
- ☐ Dk Teal - 1 skein

[4 ounces, 212 yards (113 grams, 194 meters) per skein]:

- ☐ Grey - 1 skein

Crochet Hook

- ☐ Size K (6.5 mm) **or** size needed for gauge

Additional Supplies

- ☐ Yarn needle

GAUGE INFORMATION

10 sc = 3½" (9 cm);
18 rows = 5" (12.75 cm)

Gauge Swatch: 3½" wide x 5" high (9 cm x 12.75 cm)

Work same as Solid Strip for 18 rows: 10 sc.

SOLID STRIP (Make 3)

With Off White, ch 11.

Row 1 (Right side)**:** Sc in second ch from hook and in each ch across: 10 sc.

Note: Loop a short piece of yarn around any stitch to mark Row 1 as **right** side.

Rows 2-108: Ch 1, turn; sc in each sc across.

Finish off.

6 TILES STRIP (Make 4)

For **each** Strip, work 18 rows with **each** color.

1st Strip: Dk Teal, Off White, Coral, Dk Teal, Grey and Blue/Green.

2nd Strip: Coral, Off White, Grey, Dk Teal, Blue/Green and Grey.

3rd Strip: Blue/Green, Coral, Off White, Grey, Coral and Dk Teal.

4th Strip: Dk Teal, Off White, Coral, Grey, Blue/Green and Off White.

With first color, ch 11.

Row 1 (Right side)**:** Sc in second ch from hook and in each ch across: 10 sc.

Note: Mark Row 1 as **right** side.

Rows 2-18: Ch 1, turn; sc in each sc across; at end of Row 18, change to next color in last sc ***(Fig. 3a, page 22)***.

Rows 19-36: Ch 1, turn; sc in each sc across; at end of Row 36, change to next color in last sc.

Rows 37-90: Repeat Rows 19-36, 3 times.

Rows 91-108: Ch 1, turn; sc in each sc across; at end of Row 108, finish off.

7 TILES STRIP (Make 4)

For **each** Strip, work 8 rows with first color, 18 rows for **each** of next 5 colors, then 10 rows with last color.

1st Strip: Grey, Dk Teal, Blue/Green, Off White, Blue/Green, Coral and Grey.

2nd Strip: Blue/Green, Grey, Dk Teal, Off White, Grey, Coral and Blue/Green.

3rd Strip: Off White, Dk Teal, Blue/Green, Coral, Grey, Blue/Green and Off White.

4th Strip: Coral, Grey, Off White, Blue/Green, Dk Teal, Grey and Coral.

With first color, ch 11.

Row 1 (Right side)**:** Sc in second ch from hook and in each ch across: 10 sc.

Note: Mark Row 1 as **right** side.

Rows 2-8: Ch 1, turn; sc in each sc across; at end of Row 8, change to next color in last sc.

Rows 9-26: Ch 1, turn; sc in each sc across; at end of Row 26, change to next color in last sc.

Rows 27-98: Repeat Rows 9-26, 4 times.

Rows 99-108: Ch 1, turn; sc in each sc across; at end of Row 108, finish off.

ASSEMBLY

With **right** sides of all Strips facing and using Placement Diagram as a guide, sew Strips together with corresponding colors.

PLACEMENT DIAGRAM

CONVERGING stripes

EASY +

Finished Size: 31" x 46" (78.5 cm x 117 cm)

SHOPPING LIST

Yarn (Medium Weight) 4

[6 ounces, 315 yards (170.1 grams, 288 meters) per skein]:

- ☐ MC (Off White) - 2 skeins
- ☐ Color A (Lt Blue) - 1 skein
- ☐ Color B (Dk Peach) - 1 skein
- ☐ Color C (Green) - 1 skein
- ☐ Color D (Dk Rose) - 1 skein
- ☐ Color E (Yellow) - 1 skein

Crochet Hook

- ☐ Size K (6.5 mm)
  or size needed for gauge

Additional Supplies

- ☐ Yarn needle

GAUGE INFORMATION

In pattern, 6 Blocks measured diagonally = 8½" (21.5 cm)

Each Square = 15" (38 cm)

Gauge Swatch: 6" x 6" x 8½" (15.25 cm x 15.25 cm x 21.5 cm)

With Color A, work same as Square 1 for 6 rows: 6 Blocks.

STITCH GUIDE

BEGINNING BLOCK

Ch 6, turn; dc in fourth ch from hook and in next 2 chs.

BLOCK

Slip st in ch-3 sp of next Block, ch 3, 3 dc in same sp.

SQUARE (Make 6 **total**)

Row #	1 & 2	3-6	7-10	11-15	16-19	20-23	24 & 25
Square 1	A	B	C	E	MC	D	A
Square 2	D	A	B	C	E	MC	D
Square 3	MC	D	A	B	C	E	MC
Square 4	E	MC	D	A	B	C	E
Square 5	C	E	MC	D	A	B	C
Square 6	B	C	E	MC	D	A	B

Each Square is worked diagonally from corner to corner; then 2 rounds of Border are added with MC.

Row 1 (Right side)**:** With color indicated, ch 6; dc in fourth ch from hook and in last 2 chs (**first Block made**).

Note: Loop a short piece of yarn around any stitch to mark Row 1 as **right** side.

Row 2: Work Beginning Block, slip st around beginning ch of previous Block ***(Fig. A)***, ch 3, 3 dc in same sp ***(Fig. B)*** changing to next color in last dc ***(Fig. 3b, page 22)***: 2 Blocks.

Fig. A

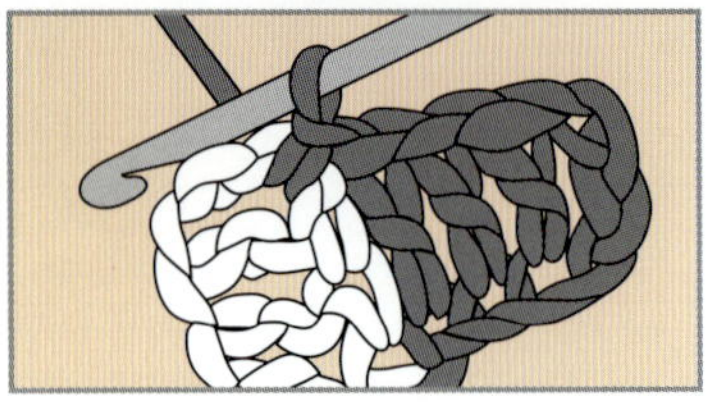

Fig. B

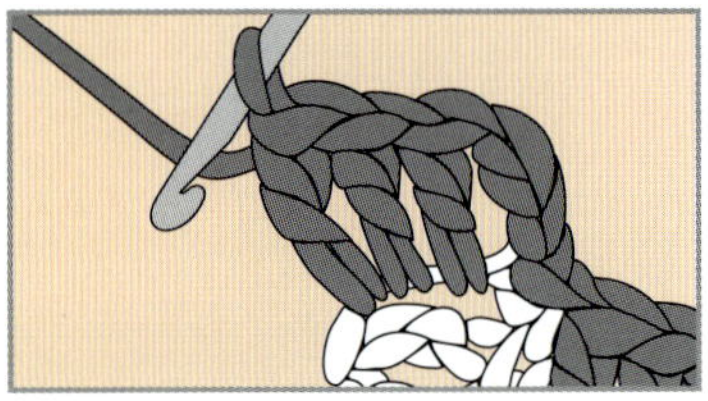

Row 3: Work Beginning Block, slip st in ch-3 sp of first Block, ch 3, 3 dc in same sp, work Block: 3 Blocks.

Rows 4-6: Work Beginning Block, slip st in ch-3 sp of first Block, ch 3, 3 dc in same sp, work Blocks across changing to next color in last dc on Row 6: 6 Blocks.

Rows 7-10: Work Beginning Block, slip st in ch-3 sp of first Block, ch 3, 3 dc in same sp, work Blocks across changing to next color in last dc on Row 10: 10 Blocks.

Rows 11-13: Work Beginning Block, slip st in ch-3 sp of first Block, ch 3, 3 dc in same sp, work Blocks across: 13 Blocks.

Rows 14 and 15: Turn; slip st in first 3 dc and in next ch-3 sp, ch 3, 3 dc in same sp, work Blocks across to last Block, slip st in ch-3 sp of last Block: 11 Blocks.

Row 16: Turn; slip st in first 3 dc, with next color, slip st in next ch-3 sp, ch 3, 3 dc in same sp, work Blocks across to last Block, slip st in ch-3 sp of last Block: 10 Blocks.

Rows 17-19: Turn; slip st in first 3 dc and in next ch-3 sp, ch 3, 3 dc in same sp, work Blocks across to last Block, slip st in ch-3 sp of last Block: 7 Blocks.

Rows 20-23: Repeat Rows 16-19: 3 Blocks.

Row 24: Turn; slip st in first 3 dc, with next color, slip st in next ch-3 sp, ch 3, 3 dc in same sp, work Block, slip st in ch-3 sp of last Block: 2 Blocks.

Row 25: Turn; slip st in first 3 dc and in next ch-3 sp, ch 3, 3 dc in same sp, slip st in ch-3 sp of last Block; finish off: one Block.

Border

Rnd 1: With **right** side facing, join MC with sc in first dc of last Block made on Row 25 ***(see Joining With Sc, page 21)***; sc in next 2 dc, 3 sc in next ch-3 sp, (sc in next 3 sts, 3 sc in next sp) around entire Square; join with slip st to first sc: 156 sc (39 sc across **each** side).

Rnd 2: Ch 3 **(counts as first dc)**, dc in same st as joining and in next 38 sc, (3 dc in next sc, dc in next 38 dc) 3 times, dc in same st as joining; join with slip st to first dc, finish off: 164 dc.

ASSEMBLY

With **wrong** sides together, using Placement Diagram as a guide, and working through **both** loops on **both** pieces, whipstitch Squares together with MC ***(Fig. 5, page 22)***, forming 2 horizontal strips of 3 Squares each, beginning in center dc of first corner and ending in center dc of next corner; then whipstitch strips together in same manner.

PLACEMENT DIAGRAM

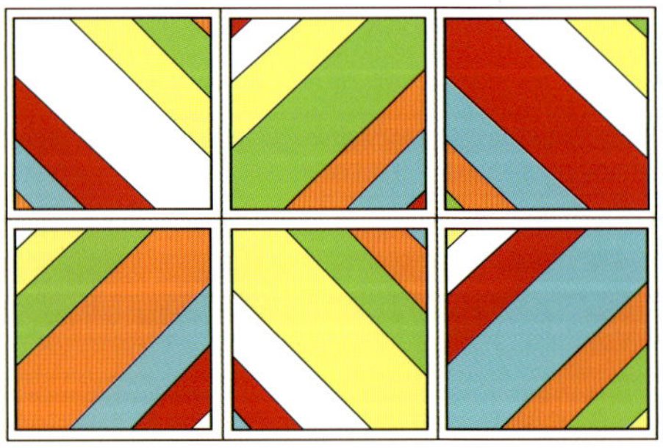

EDGING

Rnd 1: With **right** side facing, join MC with dc in any corner dc ***(see Joining With Dc, page 21)***; 2 dc in same st, ★ dc in next dc and in each dc across to center dc of next corner, 3 dc in center dc; repeat from ★ 2 times **more**, dc in next dc and in each dc across; join with slip st to first dc, finish off.

EASY

Finished Size: 28½" x 45" (72.5 cm x 114.5 cm)

STARBURST motifs

STITCH GUIDE

BEGINNING CLUSTER (uses one sp)

Ch 2, ★ YO, insert hook in sp indicated, YO and pull up a loop, YO and draw through 2 loops on hook; repeat from ★ once **more**, YO and draw through all 3 loops on hook.

CLUSTER (uses one sp)

★ YO, insert hook in sp indicated, YO and pull up a loop, YO and draw through 2 loops on hook; repeat from ★ 2 times **more**, YO and draw through all 4 loops on hook.

SHOPPING LIST

Yarn (Medium Weight) 4

[7 ounces, 370 yards (198 grams, 338 meters) per skein]:

- ☐ White - 2 skeins
- ☐ Dk Orange - 1 skein
- ☐ Gold - 1 skein
- ☐ Hot Pink - 1 skein
- ☐ Dk Teal - 1 skein

Crochet Hook

- ☐ Size K (6.5 mm) **or** size needed for gauge

Additional Supplies

- ☐ Yarn needle

GAUGE INFORMATION

Gauge Swatch: 5½" (14 cm) square

Work same as one Motif.

MOTIF (Make 40 **total**)

Make 8	Rnd 1	Rnds 2 & 3	Rnd 4
Motif A	Dk Teal	White	White
Motif B	Gold	Dk Orange	White
Motif C	Hot Pink	Dk Teal	White
Motif D	White	Gold	White
Motif E	Dk Orange	Hot Pink	White

With color indicated, ch 4; join with slip st to form a ring.

Rnd 1 (Right side)**:** Work beginning Cluster in ring, ch 2, (work Cluster in ring, ch 2) 5 times; join with slip st to top of beginning Cluster, finish off: 6 ch-2 sps.

Note: Loop a short piece of yarn around any stitch to mark Rnd 1 as **right** side.

Rnd 2: With **right** side facing, join next color with slip st in any ch-2 sp; work (beginning Cluster, ch 2, Cluster) in same sp, ch 2, (work Cluster, ch 2) twice in next ch-2 sp and in each ch-2 sp around; join with slip st to top of beginning Cluster: 12 ch-2 sps.

Rnd 3: (Slip st, work beginning Cluster) in next ch-2 sp, ch 2, work Cluster in next ch-2 sp, ch 2, (work Cluster, ch 2) twice in next ch-2 sp, ★ (work Cluster in next ch-2 sp, ch 2) twice, (work Cluster, ch 2) twice in next ch-2 sp; repeat from ★ 2 times **more**; join with slip st to top of beginning Cluster, finish off: 16 Clusters and 16 ch-2 sps.

Rnd 4: With **right** side facing, join White with sc in any corner ch-2 sp ***(see Joining With Sc, page 21)***; (sc, ch 1, 2 sc) in same sp, (sc in next Cluster, 2 sc in next ch-2 sp) 3 times, ★ (2 sc, ch 1, 2 sc) in next corner ch-2 sp, (sc in next Cluster, 2 sc in next ch-2 sp) 3 times; repeat from ★ 2 times **more**; join with slip st to first sc, finish off.

ASSEMBLY

With **wrong** sides together, using Placement Diagram as a guide, and working through **both** loops on **both** pieces, whipstitch Motifs together with White ***(Fig. 5, page 22)***, forming 5 vertical strips of 8 Motifs each, beginning in ch of first corner and ending in ch of next corner; then whipstitch strips together in same manner.

PLACEMENT DIAGRAM

A	B	C	D	E
E	A	B	C	D
D	E	A	B	C
C	D	E	A	B
B	C	D	E	A
A	B	C	D	E
E	A	B	C	D
D	E	A	B	C

EDGING

Rnd 1: With **right** side facing, join White with sc in any corner ch-1 sp; (sc, ch 1, 2 sc) in same sp, ★ sc in each st and in each joining across to next corner ch-1 sp, (2 sc, ch 1, 2 sc) in corner sp; repeat from ★ 2 times **more**, sc in each st and in each joining across; join with slip st to first sc, finish off.

Rnd 2: With **right** side facing, join Dk Orange with slip st in any corner ch-1 sp, ch 1; working from **left** to **right**, ★ insert hook in st to right of hook ***(Fig. A)***, YO and draw through, under and to left of loop on hook (2 loops on hook) ***(Fig. B)***, YO and draw through both loops on hook ***(Fig. C)*** **(reverse sc made, *Fig. D*)**; repeat from ★ around working 2 sts in each corner ch-1 sp; join with slip st to first st, finish off.

Fig. A

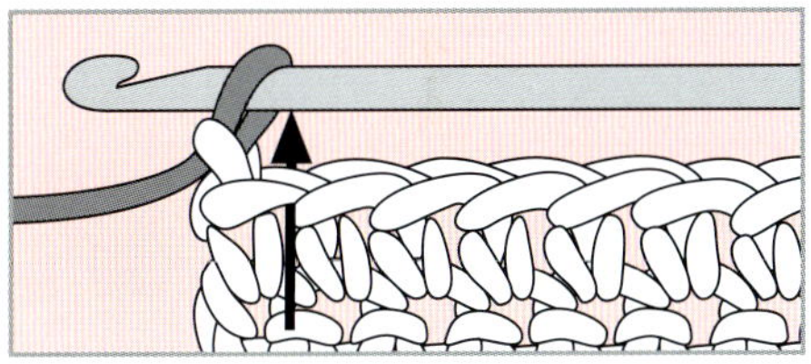

Fig. B

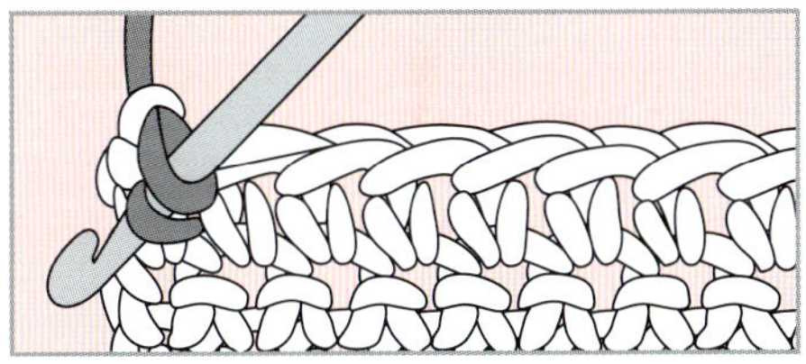

Fig. C

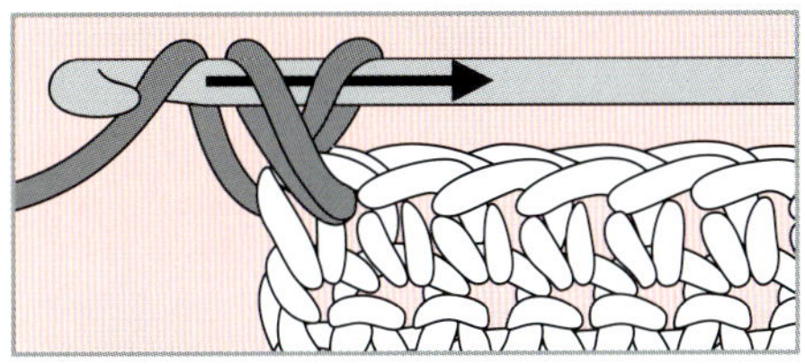

Fig. D

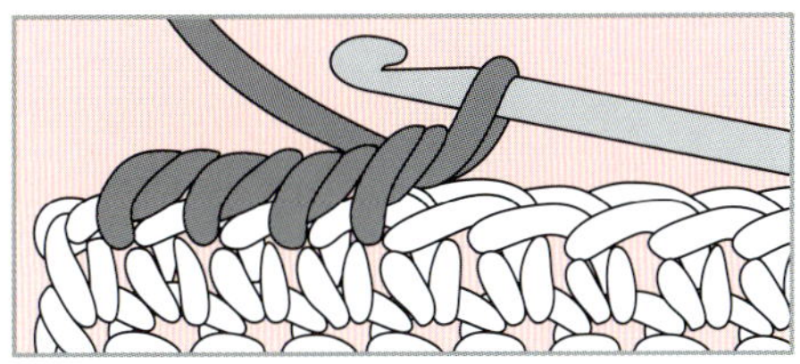

STRIPES Abloom

EASY

Finished Size: 27¼" x 44" (69 cm x 112 cm)

SHOPPING LIST

Yarn (Medium Weight) 4

[3.5 ounces, 170 yards
(100 grams, 156 meters) per skein]:

- ☐ Aqua - 2 skeins
- ☐ White - 2 skeins
- ☐ Dk Pink - 1 skein

Crochet Hook

- ☐ Size K (6.5 mm)
  or size needed for gauge

Additional Supplies

- ☐ Yarn needle

GAUGE INFORMATION

12 dc and 6 rows = 4" (10 cm)
Gauge Swatch: 4" (10 cm) square
Ch 14.
Row 1: Dc in fourth ch from hook **(3 skipped chs count as first dc)** and in each ch across: 12 dc.
Rows 2-6: Ch 3 **(counts as first dc)**, turn; dc in next dc and in each dc across.
Finish off.

Refer to Diagram, page 16, before you begin each Section.

SECTION 1

With Aqua, ch 44.

Row 1 (Right side)**:** Working in back ridge of beginning ch ***(Fig. 1, page 21)***, dc in fourth ch from hook **(3 skipped chs count as first dc)** and in each ch across changing to White in last dc ***(Fig. 3b, page 22)***: 42 dc.

Note: Loop a short piece of yarn around any stitch to mark Row 1 as **right** side.

Row 2: Ch 3 **(counts as first dc, now and throughout unless otherwise specified)**, turn; dc in next dc and in each dc across changing to Aqua in last dc.

Row 3: Ch 3, turn; dc in next dc and in each dc across changing to White in last dc.

Rows 4-13: Repeat Rows 2 and 3, 5 times.

Row 14: Ch 3, turn; dc in next dc and in each dc across changing to Dk Pink in last dc.

Rows 15-18: Ch 3, turn; dc in next dc and in each dc across.

Finish off.

SECTION 2

Row 1: With **right** side facing and working in end of Rows 1-14 of Section 1, join Dk Pink with slip st in end of Row 1; ch 3, dc in same row, 2 dc in each White and Aqua row across, do **not** work in Dk Pink rows: 28 dc.

Rows 2 and 3: Ch 3, turn; dc in next dc and in each dc across.

Row 4: Ch 3, turn; dc in next dc and in each dc across changing to Aqua in last dc.

Row 5: Ch 3, turn; dc in next dc and in each dc across changing to White in last dc.

Row 6: Ch 3, turn; dc in next dc and in each dc across changing to Aqua in last dc.

Rows 7-44: Repeat Rows 5 and 6, 19 times.

Row 45: Ch 3, turn; dc in next dc and in each dc across changing to Dk Pink.

SECTION 3

Row 1: Ch 3; with **right** side facing and working in end of rows, dc in first row, 2 dc in each White and Aqua row across, do **not** work in Dk Pink rows: 82 dc.

Rows 2 and 3: Ch 3, turn; dc in next dc and in each dc across.

Row 4: Ch 3, turn; dc in next dc and in each dc across changing to Aqua in last dc.

Row 5: Ch 3, turn; dc in next dc and in each dc across changing to White in last dc.

Row 6: Ch 3, turn; dc in next dc and in each dc across changing to Aqua in last dc.

Rows 7-26: Repeat Rows 5 and 6, 10 times.

Row 27: Ch 3, turn; dc in next dc and in each dc across changing to Dk Pink.

SECTION 4

Row 1: Ch 3; with **right** side facing and working in end of Rows 1-27 of Section 3, dc in first row, 2 dc in each row across: 54 dc.

Rows 2 and 3: Ch 3, turn; dc in next dc and in each dc across.

Row 4: Ch 3, turn; dc in next dc and in each dc across changing to Aqua in last dc.

Row 5: Ch 3, turn; dc in next 45 dc changing to White in last dc made, leave remaining 8 dc unworked: 46 dc.

Row 6: Ch 3, turn; dc in next dc and in each dc across changing to Aqua in last dc.

Row 7: Ch 3, turn; dc in next dc and in each dc across changing to White in last dc.

Rows 8-24: Repeat Rows 6 and 7, 8 times; then repeat Row 6 once **more**.

Row 25: Ch 3, turn; dc in next dc and in each dc across; finish off.

Diagram

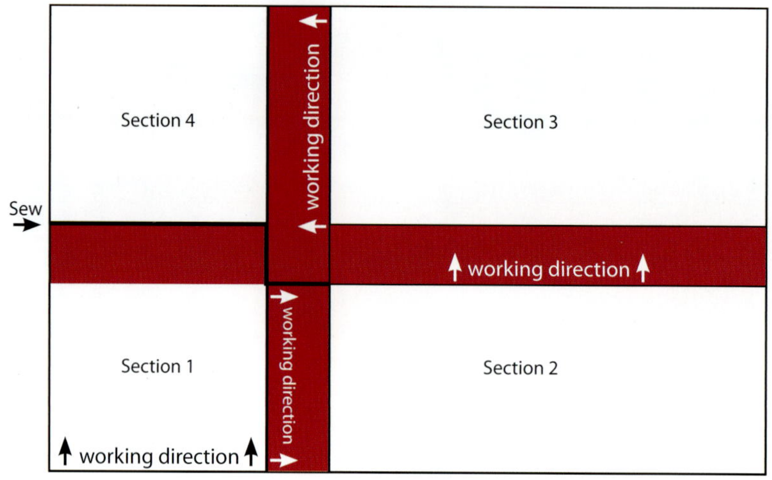

FINISHING

With Dk Pink:

Sew end of Rows 5-25 of Section 4 to top of sts on Section 1; then sew end of Rows 15-18 of Section 1 to top of unworked sts on Row 4 of Section 4.

Sew end of Rows 1-4 of Sections 2 and 4 together.

Flower

Rnd 1 (Right side)**:** With White, ch 6, (dc, ch 2) 7 times in sixth ch from hook; join with slip st to fourth ch of beginning ch-6: 8 ch-2 sps.

Note: Mark Rnd 1 as **right** side.

Rnd 2: (Slip st, ch 1, 2 dc, ch 1, slip st) in each ch-2 sp around; join with slip st to first slip st: 8 petals.

Rnd 3: Ch 3 (does **not** count as a dc), working **behind** petals, (slip st in first slip st of next petal, ch 3) around; join with slip st to same slip st as joining: 8 ch-3 sps.

Rnd 4: (Slip st, ch 1, 3 dc, ch 1, slip st) in each ch-3 sp around; join with slip st to first slip st, finish off leaving a long end for sewing.

Using photo as a guide, page 15, sew Flower to Section 4 where Dk Pink meets.

Finished Size: 35" (89 cm) square

EASY

MITERED square

SHOPPING LIST

Yarn (Medium Weight) 4

[7 ounces, 370 yards
(198 grams, 338 meters) per skein]:

- ☐ Grey - 1 skein
- ☐ White - 1 skein
- ☐ Dk Pink - 1 skein
- ☐ Green - 1 skein
- ☐ Orange - 1 skein

Crochet Hook

- ☐ Size K (6.5 mm)
  or size needed for gauge

GAUGE INFORMATION

Square = 6" (15.25 cm)
In pattern,
(3 dc, ch 1) 4 times = 5½" (14 cm);
6 rows = 4" (10 cm)
Gauge Swatch: 6" (15.25 cm) square
Work same as Square.

SQUARE

With Grey, ch 4; join with slip st to form a ring.

Rnd 1 (Wrong side)**:** Ch 3 **(counts as first dc, now and throughout)**, 2 dc in ring, ch 2, (3 dc in ring, ch 2) 3 times; join with slip st to first dc: 12 dc and 4 ch-2 sps.

Note: Loop a short piece of yarn around **back** of any stitch on Rnd 1 to mark **right** side.

Rnd 2: Slip st in next 2 dc and in next ch-2 sp, ch 3, (2 dc, ch 2, 3 dc) in same sp, ch 1, ★ (3 dc, ch 2, 3 dc) in next ch-2 sp, ch 1; repeat from ★ 2 times **more**; join with slip st to first dc: 24 dc and 8 sps.

Rnd 3: Slip st in next 2 dc and in next corner ch-2 sp, ch 3, (2 dc, ch 2, 3 dc) in same sp, ch 1, 3 dc in next ch-1 sp, ch 1, ★ (3 dc, ch 2, 3 dc) in next corner ch-2 sp, ch 1, 3 dc in next ch-1 sp, ch 1; repeat from ★ 2 times **more**; join with slip st to first dc: 36 dc and 12 sps.

Rnd 4: Slip st in next 2 dc and in next corner ch-2 sp, ch 3, (2 dc, ch 2, 3 dc) in same sp, ch 1, (3 dc in next ch-1 sp, ch 1) twice, ★ (3 dc, ch 2, 3 dc) in next corner ch-2 sp, ch 1, (3 dc in next ch-1 sp, ch 1) twice; repeat from ★ 2 times **more**; join with slip st to first dc, finish off: 48 dc and 16 sps.

BODY

Row 1: With **wrong** side facing, join White with dc in any corner ch-2 sp *(see Joining With Dc, page 21)*; dc in same sp, ch 1, (3 dc in next ch-1 sp, ch 1) across to next corner ch-2 sp, (3 dc, ch 2, 3 dc) in corner sp, ch 1, (3 dc in next ch-1 sp, ch 1) across to next corner ch-2 sp, 2 dc in corner sp, leave last 2 sides of Square unworked: 28 dc and 9 sps.

Row 2: Ch 3, turn; (3 dc in next ch-1 sp, ch 1) across to corner ch-2 sp, (3 dc, ch 2, 3 dc) in corner sp, (ch 1, 3 dc in next ch-1 sp) across to last 2 dc, skip next dc, dc in last dc: 32 dc and 9 sps.

Row 3: Ch 3, turn; dc in sp **before** next dc ***(Fig. 4, page 22)***, ch 1, (3 dc in next ch-1 sp, ch 1) across to corner ch-2 sp, (3 dc, ch 2, 3 dc) in corner sp, (ch 1, 3 dc in next ch-1 sp) across to last 4 dc, ch 1, skip next 3 dc, dc in sp **before** last dc, dc in last dc: 34 dc and 11 sps.

Row 4: Ch 3, turn; (3 dc in next ch-1 sp, ch 1) across to corner ch-2 sp, (3 dc, ch 2, 3 dc) in corner sp, (ch 1, 3 dc in next ch-1 sp) across to last 2 dc, skip next dc, dc in last dc changing to Dk Pink ***(Fig. 3b, page 22)***: 38 dc and 11 sps.

Row 5: Ch 3, turn; dc in sp **before** next dc, ch 1, (3 dc in next ch-1 sp, ch 1) across to corner ch-2 sp, (3 dc, ch 2, 3 dc) in corner sp, (ch 1, 3 dc in next ch-1 sp) across to last 4 dc, ch 1, skip next 3 dc, dc in sp **before** last dc, dc in last dc: 40 dc and 13 sps.

Row 6: Ch 3, turn; (3 dc in next ch-1 sp, ch 1) across to corner ch-2 sp, (3 dc, ch 2, 3 dc) in corner sp, (ch 1, 3 dc in next ch-1 sp) across to last 2 dc, skip next dc, dc in last dc: 44 dc and 13 sps.

Row 7: Ch 3, turn; dc in sp **before** next dc, ch 1, (3 dc in next ch-1 sp, ch 1) across to corner ch-2 sp, (3 dc, ch 2, 3 dc) in corner sp, (ch 1, 3 dc in next ch-1 sp) across to last 4 dc, ch 1, skip next 3 dc, dc in sp **before** last dc, dc in last dc: 46 dc and 15 sps.

Row 8: Ch 3, turn; (3 dc in next ch-1 sp, ch 1) across to corner ch-2 sp, (3 dc, ch 2, 3 dc) in corner sp, (ch 1, 3 dc in next ch-1 sp) across to last 2 dc, skip next dc, dc in last dc changing to Green: 50 dc and 15 sps.

Rows 9-32: Repeat Rows 5-8, 6 times changing color at end of **each** Row 8 in the following color sequence: Orange, White, Dk Pink, Green, Orange, White: 122 dc and 39 sps.

Row 33: Ch 3, turn; dc in sp **before** next dc, ch 1, (3 dc in next ch-1 sp, ch 1) across to corner ch-2 sp, (3 dc, ch 2, 3 dc) in corner sp, (ch 1, 3 dc in next ch-1 sp) across to last 4 dc, ch 1, skip next 3 dc, dc in sp **before** last dc, dc in last dc: 124 dc and 41 sps.

Row 34: Ch 3, turn; (3 dc in next ch-1 sp, ch 1) across to corner ch-2 sp, (3 dc, ch 2, 3 dc) in corner sp, (ch 1, 3 dc in next ch-1 sp) across to last 2 dc, skip next dc, dc in last dc changing to Dk Pink: 128 dc and 41 sps.

Rows 35-40: Repeat Rows 33 and 34, 3 times changing color at end of **each** Row 34 in the following color sequence: Green, Orange, Grey: 146 dc and 47 sps.

Row 41: Ch 3, turn; dc in sp **before** next dc, ch 1, (3 dc in next ch-1 sp, ch 1) across to corner ch-2 sp, (3 dc, ch 2, 3 dc) in corner sp, (ch 1, 3 dc in next ch-1 sp) across to last 4 dc, ch 1, skip next 3 dc, dc in sp **before** last dc, dc in last dc: 148 dc and 49 sps.

Row 42: Ch 3, turn; (3 dc in next ch-1 sp, ch 1) across to corner ch-2 sp, (3 dc, ch 2, 3 dc) in corner sp, (ch 1, 3 dc in next ch-1 sp) across to last 2 dc, skip next dc, dc in last dc; finish off: 152 dc and 49 sps.

GENERAL INSTRUCTIONS

ABBREVIATIONS

ch(s)	chain(s)
cm	centimeters
dc	double crochet(s)
MC	Main Color
mm	millimeters
Rnd(s)	Round(s)
sc	single crochet(s)
sp(s)	space(s)
st(s)	stitch(es)
YO	yarn over

SYMBOLS & TERMS

★ — work instructions following ★ as many **more** times as indicated in addition to the first time.

† to † — work all instructions from first † to second † **as many** times as specified.

CROCHET TERMINOLOGY		
UNITED STATES		INTERNATIONAL
slip stitch (slip st)	=	single crochet (sc)
single crochet (sc)	=	double crochet (dc)
half double crochet (hdc)	=	half treble crochet (htr)
double crochet (dc)	=	treble crochet (tr)
treble crochet (tr)	=	double treble crochet (dtr)
double treble crochet (dtr)	=	triple treble crochet (ttr)
triple treble crochet (tr tr)	=	quadruple treble crochet (qtr)
skip	=	miss

( ) or **[ ]** — work enclosed instructions **as many** times as specified by the number immediately following **or** work all enclosed instructions in the stitch or space indicated **or** contains explanatory remarks.

colon (:) — the number(s) given after a colon at the end of a row or round denote(s) the number of stitches or spaces you should have on that row or round.

BEGINNER	Projects for first-time crocheters using basic stitches. Minimal shaping.
EASY	Projects using yarn with basic stitches, repetitive stitch patterns, simple color changes, and simple shaping and finishing.
INTERMEDIATE	Projects using a variety of techniques, such as basic lace patterns or color patterns, mid-level shaping and finishing.
EXPERIENCED	Projects with intricate stitch patterns, techniques and dimension, such as non-repeating patterns, multi-color techniques, fine threads, small hooks, detailed shaping and refined finishing.

CROCHET HOOKS																	
U.S.	B-1	C-2	D-3	E-4	F-5	G-6	7	H-8	I-9	J-10	K-10½	L-11	M/N-13	N/P-15	P/Q	Q	S
Metric - mm	2.25	2.75	3.25	3.5	3.75	4	4.5	5	5.5	6	6.5	8	9	10	15	16	19

GAUGE

Exact gauge is **essential** for proper size. Before beginning your project, make the sample swatch given in the individual instructions in the yarn and hook specified. After completing the swatch, measure it, counting your stitches and rows/rounds carefully. If your swatch is larger or smaller than specified, **make another, changing hook size to get the correct gauge**. Keep trying until you find the size hook that will give you the specified gauge.

JOINING WITH SC

When instructed to join with sc, begin with a slip knot on the hook. Insert the hook in the stitch or space indicated, YO and pull up a loop, YO and draw through both loops on hook.

JOINING WITH DC

When instructed to join with dc, begin with a slip knot on the hook. YO, holding loop on hook, insert the hook in the stitch or space indicated, YO and pull up a loop (3 loops on hook), (YO and draw through 2 loops on hook) twice.

BACK RIDGE

Work only in loops indicated by arrows ***(Fig. 1)***.

Fig. 1

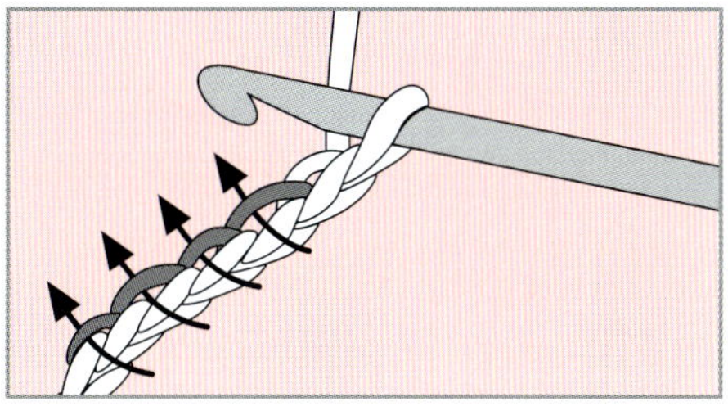

FREE LOOPS OF A CHAIN

When instructed to work in free loops of a chain, work in loop indicated by arrow ***(Fig. 2)***.

Fig. 2

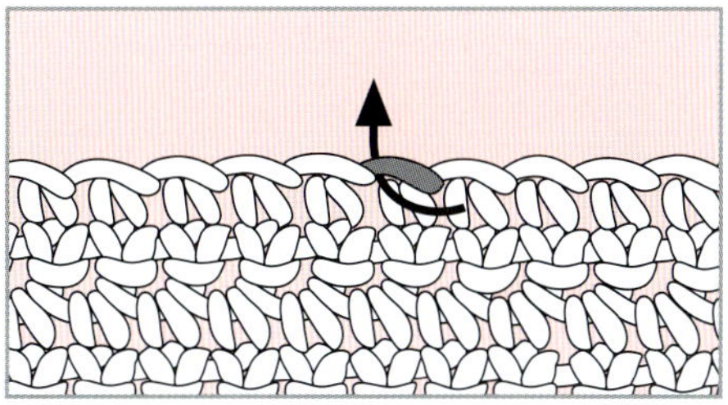

Yarn Weight Symbol & Names	LACE 0	SUPER FINE 1	FINE 2	LIGHT 3	MEDIUM 4	BULKY 5	SUPER BULKY 6	JUMBO 7
Type of Yarns in Category	Fingering, size 10 crochet thread	Sock, Fingering, Baby	Sport, Baby	DK, Light Worsted	Worsted, Afghan, Aran	Chunky, Craft, Rug	Super Bulky, Roving	Jumbo, Roving
Crochet Gauge* Ranges in Single Crochet to 4" (10 cm)	32-42 sts**	21-32 sts	16-20 sts	12-17 sts	11-14 sts	8-11 sts	6-9 sts	5 sts and fewer
Advised Hook Size Range	Steel*** 6 to 8, Regular hook B-1	B-1 to E-4	E-4 to 7	7 to I-9	I-9 to K-10½	K-10½ to M/N-13	M/N-13 to Q	Q and larger

*GUIDELINES ONLY: The chart above reflects the most commonly used gauges and hook sizes for specific yarn categories.

** Lace weight yarns are usually crocheted with larger hooks to create lacy openwork patterns. Accordingly, a gauge range is difficult to determine. Always follow the gauge stated in your pattern.

*** Steel crochet hooks are sized differently from regular hooks–the higher the number, the smaller the hook, which is the reverse of regular hook sizing.

CHANGING COLORS

Work the last stitch to within one step of completion (2 loops on hook), hook new yarn ***(Fig. 3a or 3b)*** and draw through both loops on hook. Cut old yarn and work over both ends.

Fig. 3a

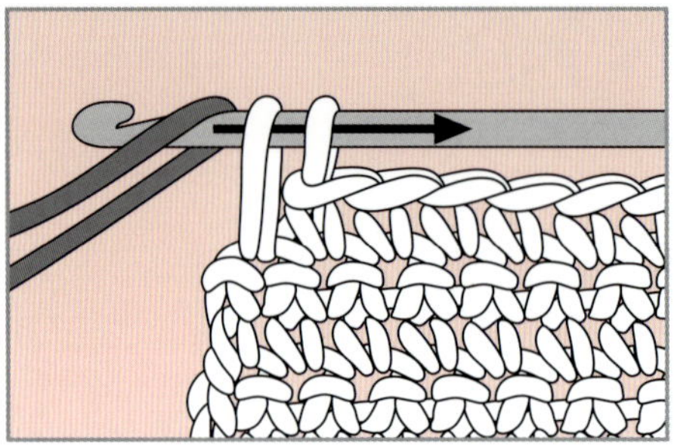

Fig. 3b

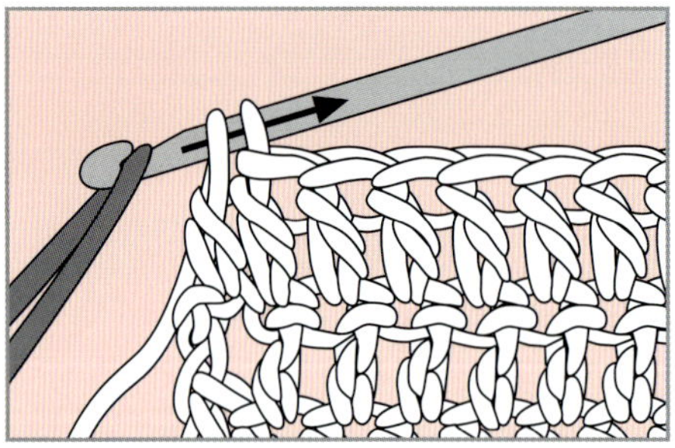

WORKING IN A SPACE BEFORE A STITCH

When instructed to work in space **before** a stitch or in spaces **between** stitches, insert hook in space indicated by arrow ***(Fig. 4)***.

Fig. 4

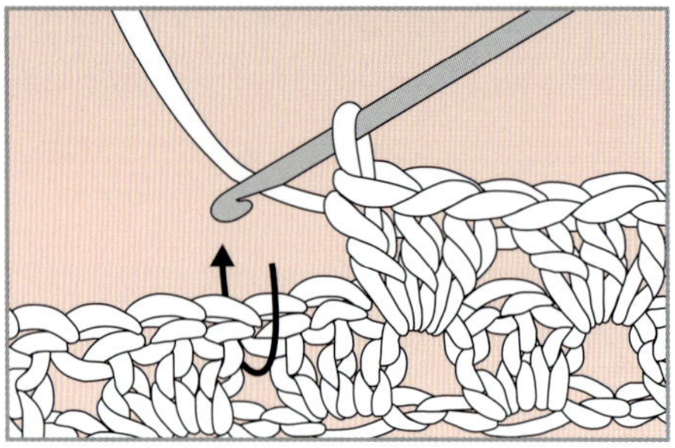

WHIPSTITCH

Place two Squares with **wrong** sides together. Beginning in center of corner, sew through both pieces once to secure the beginning of the seam, leaving an ample yarn end to weave in later. Insert the needle from **front** to **back** through **both** loops on **both** pieces ***(Fig. 5)***. Bring the needle around and insert it from **front** to **back** through next loops of both pieces. Continue in this manner across to center of next corner, keeping the sewing yarn fairly loose.

Fig. 5

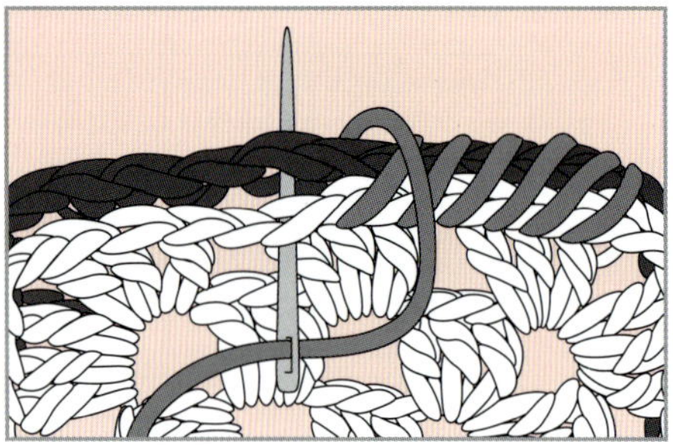

YARN INFORMATION

Each Blanket in this book was made using Medium Weight Yarn. Any brand of Medium Weight Yarn may be used. It is best to refer to the yardage/meters when determining how many balls or skeins to purchase. Remember, to arrive at the finished size, it is the GAUGE/TENSION that is important, not the brand of yarn.

For your convenience, listed below are the specific yarns used to create our photography models. Because yarn manufacturers make frequent changes in their product lines, you may sometimes find it necessary to use substitute yarn or to search for the discontinued product at alternate suppliers (locally or online).

NINE-COLOR COMBO

Caron® Simply Soft®

Dk Rose - #9764 Fuchsia
Strawberry - #0015 Strawberry
Purple - #9781 Purple
Off White - #9702 Off White
Lavender - #9717 Orchid
Blue - #9784 Cobalt Blue
Lime Green - #9771 Chartreuse
Dk Peach - #9754 Persimmon
Yellow - #9755 Sunshine

COLORFUL SUBWAY

Red Heart® Soft®

Off White - #4601 Off White
Blue/Green - #9520 Seafoam
Coral - #9251 Coral
Dk Teal - #9518 Teal
Grey - #9440 Lt Grey Heather

CONVERGING STRIPES

Caron® Simply Soft®

Off White - #9702 Off White
Lt Blue - #9780 Robins Egg
Dk Peach - #9754 Persimmon
Green - #0003 Pistachio
Dk Rose - #9764 Fuchsia
Yellow - #9755 Sunshine

STARBURST MOTIFS

Red Heart® With Love®

White - #1001 White
Dk Orange - #1252 Mango
Gold - #1207 Cornsilk
Hot Pink - #1701 Hot Pink
Dk Teal - #1623 Mallard

STRIPES ABLOOM

Lion Brand® Vanna's Choice®

Aqua - #102 Aqua
White - #100 White
Dk Pink - #112 Raspberry

MITERED SQUARE

Red Heart® With Love®

Grey - #1401 Pewter
White - #1001 White
Dk Pink - #1939 Papaya
Green - #1562 Jadeite
Orange - #1252 Mango

MEET kristi simpson

Inspired by her love of yarn, Kristi Simpson creates crochet and knit patterns with a fresh and modern touch. The mother of five became hooked on crochet after teaching herself so she could help her daughter make a scarf from a "learn to crochet" kit that was a gift.

"I loved it from the beginning," she says. "I was amazed that I could take a string of yarn and create something so useful and pretty! Needless to say, I never stopped!"

Other Leisure Arts books featuring Kristi's designs include Rucksacks and Backpacks (#7058), Lacy Wraps (#6995), Urban Slouch Hats (#6796), Easy Essential Bags (#6795), Animal Baby Bibs (#6850), Animal Blankets (#6996), Sweet and Sporty Diaper Covers (#6719), and Modern Baby Booties (#6914). Visit kristisimpson.net or find her on Ravelry, Facebook, and Pinterest.

Production Team: Instructional/Technical Editor - Linda A. Daley; Editorial Writer - Susan Frantz Wiles; Senior Graphic Artist - Lora Puls; Graphic Artists - Leia Morshedi and Kellie McAnulty; Photo Stylist - Lori Wenger; and Photographer - Jason Masters.